D1256075

TRUST ME, HANSEL AND GRETEL ARE *SWEET!*

The Story of HANSEL AND GRETEL

as Told by THE WITCH

by Nancy Loewen

illustrated by Janna Bock

PICTURE WINDOW BOOKS
a capstone imprint

Special thanks to our adviser, Terry Flaherty, PhD, Professor of English,
Minnesota State University, Mankato, for his expertise.

Editor: Jill Kalz
Designer: Ted Williams
Creative Director: Nathan Gassman
Production Specialist: Jennifer Walker
The illustrations in this book were created digitally.

Picture Window Books
1710 Roe Crest Drive
North Mankato, MN 56003
www.mycapstone.com

Library of Congress Cataloging-in-Publication Data
Cataloging-in-publication information is on file with the Library of Congress.
ISBN 978-1-4795-8623-3 (library binding)
ISBN 978-1-4795-8627-1 (paperback)
ISBN 978-1-4795-8631-8 (eBook PDF)

Printed and bound in China.
092015   007515LEOS16

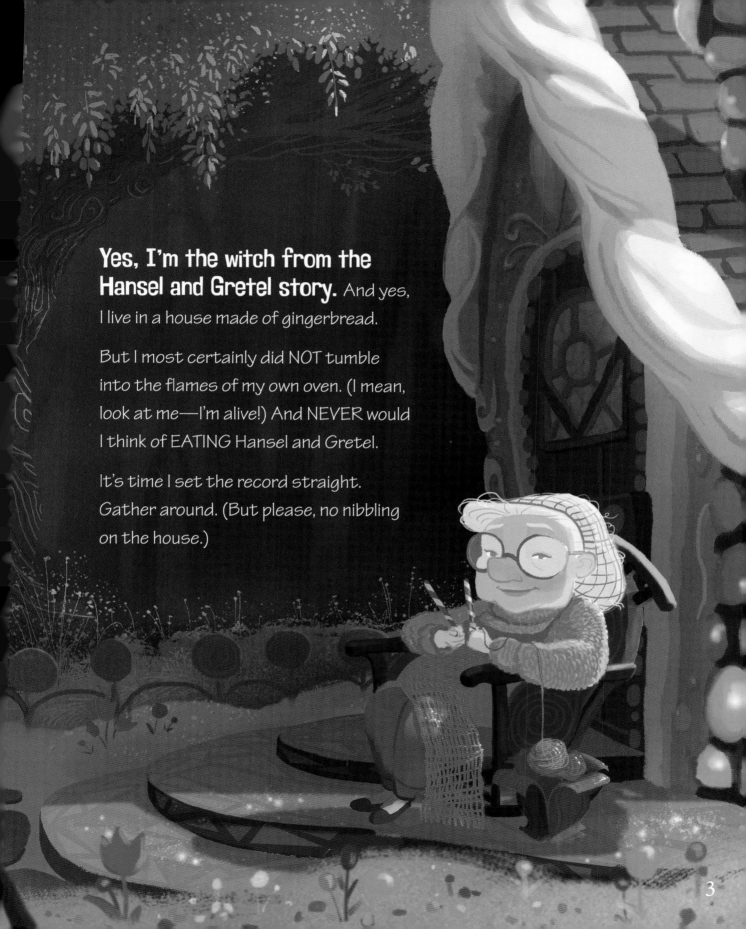

Yes, I'm the witch from the Hansel and Gretel story. And yes, I live in a house made of gingerbread.

But I most certainly did NOT tumble into the flames of my own oven. (I mean, look at me—I'm alive!) And NEVER would I think of EATING Hansel and Gretel.

It's time I set the record straight. Gather around. (But please, no nibbling on the house.)

I always knew I was different. While the other little witches were learning to make potions and cast spells, I was playing with my food. I molded mashed potatoes into polar bears. I wove noodles into wall hangings.

4

As I grew up, my projects got bigger and better. I was a food artist! I made beds out of marshmallows and floors out of rock candy. Eventually I built my own cottage. **My masterpiece.**

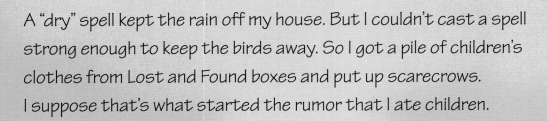

A "dry" spell kept the rain off my house. But I couldn't cast a spell strong enough to keep the birds away. So I got a pile of children's clothes from Lost and Found boxes and put up scarecrows. I suppose that's what started the rumor that I ate children.

The scarecrows did the trick—except for one crow who wasn't the least bit scared. I called him Thorn. Every day I had to patch the messes he'd make. It was an ongoing battle.

Not long ago I was in back doing touch-up work when I heard children's voices. A shutter snapped. A window shattered.

Little hooligans were eating my house!

I ran around to the front. "Stop that this instant!" I yelled. "This is private property!"

The children, a boy and a girl, stared at me in horror.

"We're sorry!" said the girl. "But we're so hungry!"

"Please don't eat us!" the boy begged.

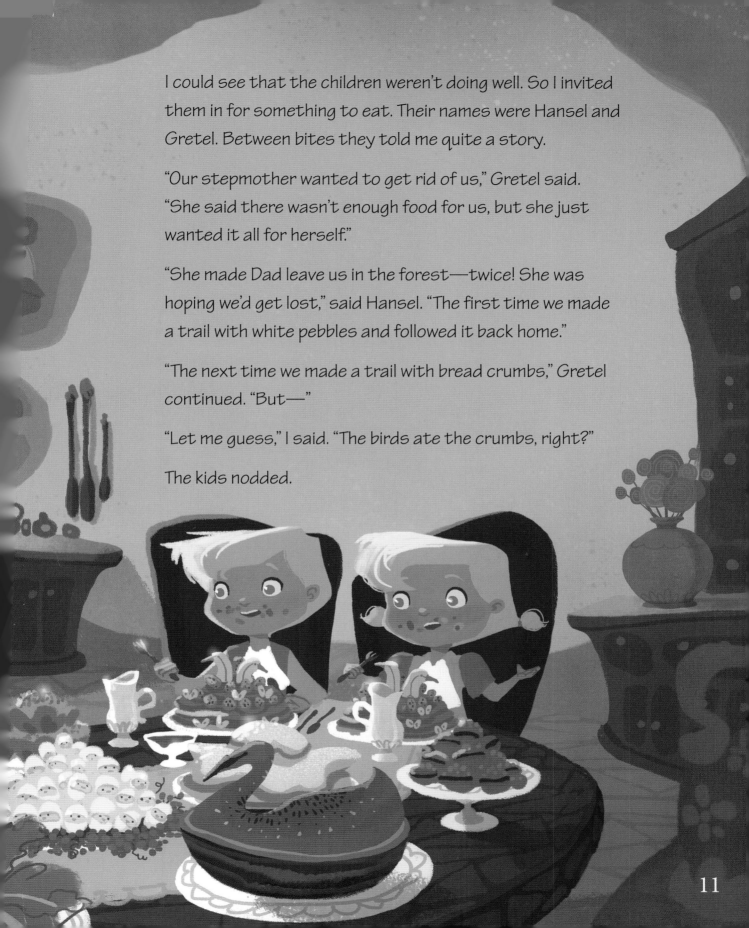

I could see that the children weren't doing well. So I invited them in for something to eat. Their names were Hansel and Gretel. Between bites they told me quite a story.

"Our stepmother wanted to get rid of us," Gretel said. "She said there wasn't enough food for us, but she just wanted it all for herself."

"She made Dad leave us in the forest—twice! She was hoping we'd get lost," said Hansel. "The first time we made a trail with white pebbles and followed it back home."

"The next time we made a trail with bread crumbs," Gretel continued. "But—"

"Let me guess," I said. "The birds ate the crumbs, right?"

The kids nodded.

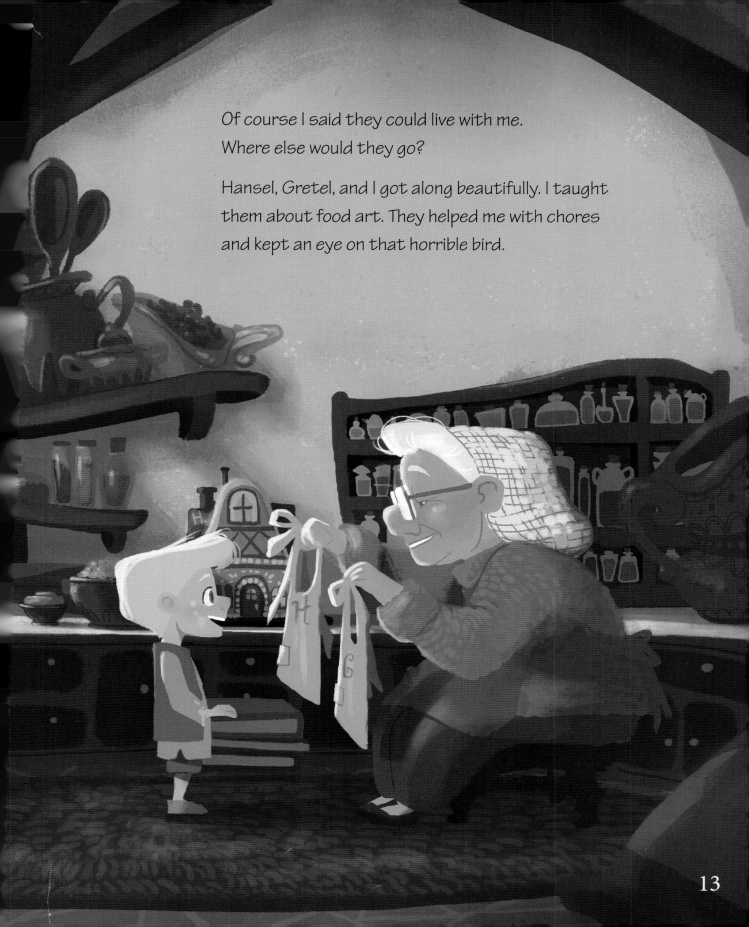

Of course I said they could live with me.
Where else would they go?

Hansel, Gretel, and I got along beautifully. I taught them about food art. They helped me with chores and kept an eye on that horrible bird.

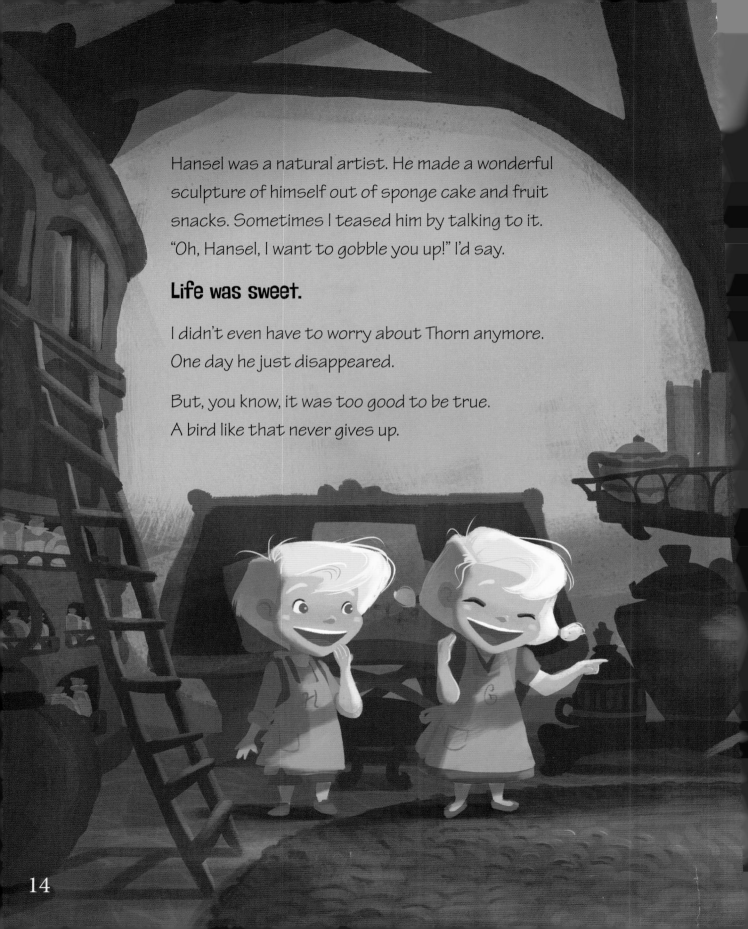

Hansel was a natural artist. He made a wonderful sculpture of himself out of sponge cake and fruit snacks. Sometimes I teased him by talking to it. "Oh, Hansel, I want to gobble you up!" I'd say.

Life was sweet.

I didn't even have to worry about Thorn anymore. One day he just disappeared.

But, you know, it was too good to be true. A bird like that never gives up.

A few weeks later, the kids and I were baking pies. Suddenly
Thorn landed on my window box and began pecking away.
Then a woman's voice called,

"Yoo-hoo! Is anyone home?"

Hansel and Gretel turned as white as powdered sugar.
Their wicked stepmother!

17

Yes, the stepmother and Thorn were working together! They wanted the kids and me out of the picture so they could eat my house. Well, THAT wasn't going to happen.

I flung open the door. "Now look here," I began, but the woman pushed past me.

"Darling children, you're alive!" she exclaimed.

"Run for it!" I told Hansel and Gretel.

I grabbed a pie and was about to throw it in the stepmother's face—when she opened the oven door and shoved me in!

(I know this is a very scary part of the story. If you need to take a few deep breaths, go ahead.)

19

So there I was, hollering and pounding on the oven door.
But then I realized something: The flames weren't burning
me. In fact they tickled.

**My dear old oven, my true and best friend,
would NEVER harm me.**

When the stepmother checked to see if I'd burned to a crisp, out I popped. Not a toasted hair on my head!

She ran away, shrieking. Thorn flew close behind. They were never heard from again.

Now life is even sweeter. Hansel and Gretel still live with me. So does their dad—a nice fellow, now that his wicked wife isn't around.

With all these extra helping hands, I've made plans to expand. A guest house … a playroom … maybe a swimming pool. We'll have a party when it's all finished. **YOU will most certainly be invited!**

Critical Thinking Using the Common Core

Look online to find the original "Hansel and Gretel" story. Describe how the character of the witch looks and acts. Compare and contrast her with the witch in this version of the story. (Integration of Knowledge and Ideas)

Rain and hungry visitors mean trouble for the witch's gingerbread house. Explain how the witch tries to keep her cottage safe. Which methods work? Which methods don't work? (Key Ideas and Details)

If Thorn told the story instead of the witch, what details might he tell differently? What if Hansel told the story? How would his point of view differ? (Craft and Structure)

Thorn is a character who doesn't speak, and yet his actions are an important part of the plot. What do the illustrations tell you about Thorn? (Integration of Knowledge and Ideas)

Glossary

character—a person, animal, or creature in a story
plot—what happens in a story
point of view—a way of looking at something
version—an account of something from a certain point of view

Read More

Duffy, Chris, ed. *Fairy Tale Comics*. New York: First Second, 2013.

Gaiman, Neil. *Hansel & Gretel: A Toon Graphic*. New York: Toon Graphics, 2014.

Yolen, Jane, and Rebecca Kai Dotlich. *Grumbles from the Forest: Fairy-Tale Voices with a Twist*. Honesdale, Penn.: WordSong, 2013.

Internet Sites

FactHound offers a safe, fun way to find Internet sites related to this book. All of the sites on FactHound have been researched by our staff.

Here's all you do:
Visit *www.facthound.com*
Type in this code: 9781479586233

Look for all the books in the series:

Believe Me, Goldilocks Rocks!
Believe Me, I Never Felt a Pea!
Frankly, I'd Rather Spin Myself a New Name!
Frankly, I Never Wanted to Kiss Anybody!
Honestly, Red Riding Hood Was Rotten!
No Kidding, Mermaids Are a Joke!
No Lie, I Acted Like a Beast!

No Lie, Pigs (and Their Houses) CAN Fly!
Really, Rapunzel Needed a Haircut!
Seriously, Cinderella Is SO Annoying!
Seriously, Snow White Was SO Forgetful!
Truly, We Both Loved Beauty Dearly!
Trust Me, Hansel and Gretel Are SWEET!
Trust Me, Jack's Beanstalk Stinks!

Super-cool stuff! Check out projects, games and lots more at www.capstonekids.com